Blackie's Self-Learning English Series

Self-Learning English Course with Activities

1

This Series is developed to promote Learning, Speaking and Writing Correct English as per Guidelines provided by CBSE under CCE pattern

Edited By
RITA WILSON
Former Principal Auckland House School, Shimla
Former Principal Starex International School, Gurgaon
&
Former Officiating Chief Executive & Secretary Council for the Indian School Certificate Examinations (CISCE), New Delhi

Authors

KALPANA AGGARWAL
M.A., B.Ed.
S.R.D.A.V. Public School
Dayanand Vihar, Delhi

MILAN GOWEL
B.A., B.Ed.
S.R.D.A.V. Public School
Dayanand Vihar, Delhi

BLACKIE
ELT BOOKS
(An imprint of S. Chand Publishing)

BLACKIE ELT BOOKS
(An imprint of S. Chand Publishing)
A Division of S. Chand And Company Pvt. Ltd.
(An ISO 9001 : 2008 Company)
7361, Ram Nagar, Qutab Road, New Delhi-110055
Phone: 23672080-81-82, 9899107446, 9911310888; Fax: 91-11-23677446
www.schandpublishing.com; e-mail : helpdesk@schandpublishing.com

Branches :

Ahmedabad	:	Ph: 27541965, 27542369, ahmedabad@schandpublishing.com
Bengaluru	:	Ph: 22268048, 22354008, bangalore@schandpublishing.com
Bhopal	:	Ph: 4274723, 4209587, bhopal@schandpublishing.com
Chandigarh	:	Ph: 2725443, 2725446, chandigarh@schandpublishing.com
Chennai	:	Ph: 28410027, 28410058, chennai@schandpublishing.com
Coimbatore	:	Ph: 2323620, 4217136, coimbatore@schandpublishing.com (Marketing Office)
Cuttack	:	Ph: 2332580; 2332581, cuttack@schandpublishing.com
Dehradun	:	Ph: 2711101, 2710861, dehradun@schandpublishing.com
Guwahati	:	Ph: 2738811, 2735640, guwahati@schandpublishing.com
Hyderabad	:	Ph: 27550194, 27550195, hyderabad@schandpublishing.com
Jaipur	:	Ph: 2219175, 2219176, jaipur@schandpublishing.com
Jalandhar	:	Ph: 2401630, 5000630, jalandhar@schandpublishing.com
Kochi	:	Ph: 2378740, 2378207-08, cochin@schandpublishing.com
Kolkata	:	Ph: 22367459, 22373914, kolkata@schandpublishing.com
Lucknow	:	Ph: 4026791, 4065646, lucknow@schandpublishing.com
Mumbai	:	Ph: 22690881, 22610885, mumbai@schandpublishing.com
Nagpur	:	Ph: 6451311, 2720523, 2777666, nagpur@schandpublishing.com
Patna	:	Ph: 2300489, 2302100, patna@schandpublishing.com
Pune	:	Ph: 64017298, pune@schandpublishing.com
Raipur	:	Ph: 2443142, raipur@schandpublishing.com (Marketing Office)
Ranchi	:	Ph: 2361178, ranchi@schandpublishing.com
Siliguri	:	Ph: 2520750, siliguri@schandpublishing.com (Marketing Office)
Visakhapatnam	:	Ph: 2782609, visakhapatnam@schandpublishing.com (Marketing Office)

First Published in 2009
Second Revised Edition 2015
Reprints 2010, 2011, 2012, 2013, 2014, 2016 (Twice)

ISBN : 978-81-219-3129-8 **Code :** 1011D 1067

PRINTED IN INDIA
By Vikas Publishing House Pvt. Ltd., Plot 20/4, Site-IV, Industrial Area Sahibabad, Ghaziabad-201010
and Published by S. Chand And Company Pvt. Ltd., 7361, Ram Nagar, New Delhi -110 055.

Preface

Communication is life. Just as healthy biological life is possible only when the brain is able to communicate well with other parts of the body, similarly a successful social life is possible when one is able to communicate well with other members of society.

Self-Learning English Course with Activities is a series of ten books that is especially designed for primary classes, keeping in view the latest trends of Communicative Teaching of English Language. The aim of this series is to help the learner attain Communicative Competence in the English language. The practice material includes Comprehension Passages and Interactive Exercises. There are also activities designed to stimulate children to think and develop their creative powers. Through these books students take on a less heavy structural load but come away with greater language ability and confidence.

Language is a means of communication. How effectively one communicates and interacts with people reflects ones personality. Interaction and Communication skills need development right from an early stage. Keeping this in mind the Central Board of Secondary Education has formulated and introduced a stepwise scheme of Communicative Approach as a part of the teaching of English as a language. Based on the guidelines, an effort has been made to provide suitable practice material on comprehension passages and writing skills while taking care of Grammar. Thus the old adage 'Practice makes a man perfect' has been implemented. The development of material is from the simple to the complex in a carefully graded manner with suitable practice exercises.

We extend our grateful thanks to the entire management and editorial staff of S. Chand and Co. Pvt. Ltd., who took great pains to get the book published in an attractive format.

The authors invite constructive feedback from teachers and users which will be thankfully acknowledged in the future editions of the book.

Authors

Acknowledgment

Rodney Bennett for 'My Dog, Spot'; Arnold Shapiro for "I Speak, I Say, I Talk".

Although every effort has been made to contact the owners of copyright of the pieces published here, a few have been impossible to trace. If they could please contact the publishers, appropriate acknowledgement will be made in future editions.

Contents

Comprehension of Unseen Passages and Poems

An Example from Prose

The Festival of Lights ________ 1

An Example from Poetry

The Spring ________ 2

Comprehension 3 – 22

1. A Birthday Gift ________ 3
2. The Crows and the Snake ________ 5
3. Riddhima and her Doll ________ 7
4. The Frogs and the Boys ________ 9
5. The Tenth Boy ________ 11
6. The Emperor's New Clothes ________ 13
7. My Dog, Spot ________ 15
8. The Kitten ________ 17
9. My Computer ________ 19
10. The Funny World ________ 21

Grammar 23 – 72

11. The Sentence ________ 23
12. Naming Words (Nouns) ________ 25

13. One and Many (Singular and Plural) 29
14. Animals–Their Homes and Sounds 33
15. Jack and Jill (Gender) 36
16. Special Names (Proper Nouns) 38
17. A and An 40
18. This and That, These and Those 43
19. Opposites 47
20. Action Words (Verb) 51
21. 'Was' and 'Were' 57
22. 'Has' and 'Have' 58
23. The Right Word 59
24. Words used in Place of Nouns (Pronouns) 60
25. Word Puzzle 63
26. Describing Words (Adjectives) 65
27. In What Position? (Preposition) 70
28. Riddles 73
29. Creative Writing 74
30. Picture Composition 77

Comprehension of Unseen Passages and Poems

An Example from Prose

The Festival of Lights

Read the passage:

Diwali is one of the most important festivals of the Hindus. It is called the 'Festival of Lights'. Men, women and children are full of joy. People wear beautiful clothes. Children go to shop with their parents. They buy toys and sweets. People light hundreds of lamps and candles in the evening. People worship Lakshmi, the goddess of wealth. They pray to her to give them wealth and health. People decorate their houses with rangoli. Children play with crackers.

Read the questions along with the answers:

1. What do children do on Diwali?

Ans. Children buy toys and crackers on Diwali. They even wear new clothes.

2. Why do people worship Goddess Lakshmi on Diwali?

Ans. People worship Goddess Lakshmi to give them wealth and health.

3. Find a word from the passage which means the same as :

   a. delighted **happy**

   b. to pray **worship**

   c. to burn **light**

4. Fill the blanks with suitable words from the passage :

   a. Children go to shop with their **parents**.

   b. People pray to Lakshmi to give **health** and **wealth**.

   c. People decorate their houses with **candles, decorative lights, rangoli.**

   d. Diwali is an important festival of the **Hindus**.

An Example from Poetry

The Spring

Read the poem:

I'm very glad that Spring has come ;
The sun shines so bright ;
Little birds upon the trees
Are singing with delight.

The young grass looks so fresh and green ;
The young lambs sport and play ;
And I can skip and run about
As merrily as they.

Read the questions along with the answers:

1. Why is the poet glad?

Ans. **The poet is glad because it is the spring season.**

2. How does the sun shine in spring season?

Ans. **The sun shines brightly in the spring season.**

3. What are the little birds doing?

Ans. **The little birds are singing with delight.**

4. Fill the blanks :-

   a. The grass looks **fresh** and **green**.

   b. The young lambs **dance** and play.

5. What does `they' in the last line stand for?

Ans. **'They' stands for the lambs in the last line.**

6. What rhymes with –

   Play **they** Bright **delight**

7. Pick words from the poem which describe the following nouns.

   a. **bright** sun **b.** **little** birds **c.** **young** lambs

1 A Birthday Gift

Read the passage and answer the questions that follow:

Sahil wanted a bicycle for his sixth birthday. His father had no money. Sahil was sad but he did not complain.

One day Sahil was returning from school. He saw a big boy riding a small bicycle. It was funny to see a big boy on a small bicycle. Suddenly Sahil heard a crash. He ran to see what it was. He found the big boy lying on the ground. The boy was hurt. He said, 'I am Wasiq. Could you please take me to my house? It is just down the road.'

'Sure,' said Sahil. They reached Wasiq's home. Wasiq's parents thanked Sahil.

The next day Sahil went to Wasiq's house to see how he was. Wasiq was fine.

Wasiq asked Sahil, 'Do you have a bicycle?'

'No,' said Sahil.

'My father said you can have mine. It is too small for me. He is buying me a big one for my birthday next week.' said Wasiq.

Sahil was very happy. He said, 'Thank you very much.'

'Will you come to my birthday party?' asked Wasiq.

'I will be the first at the birthday party!' said Sahil.

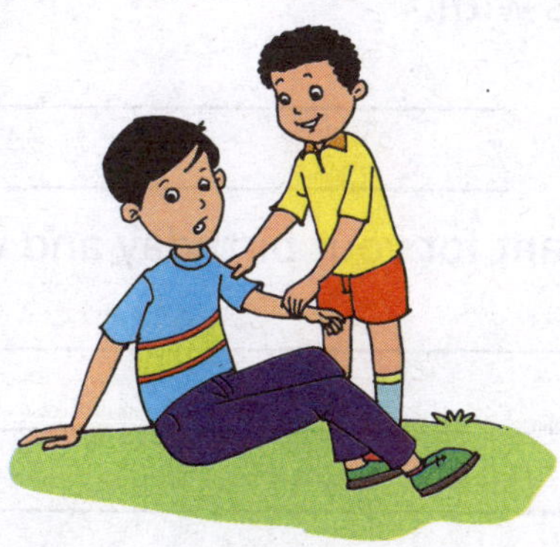

Questions

1. Tick [✓] the right answer:

A. Sahil wanted a _____________ on his birthday.

a. a car **b.** a game **c.** a bat **d.** a bicycle

B. What did Wasiq want to give Sahil.

a. a big bicycle **b.** a small bicycle

c. a new story book **d.** games on CD

C. Wasiq asked Sahil to take him _____________

a. to the hospital **b.** to play **c.** to the doctor **d.** to his home

2. Write true [T] or false [F] –

A. It was Sahil's sixth birthday. [ ]

B. Sahil visited Wasiq to find out how he was. [ ]

C. Wasiq's parents scolded Sahil. [ ]

D. Wasiq did not invite Sahil for his birthday. [ ]

3. Sahil saw something funny one day. What was it?

Ans. ____

____

4. What had happened to Wasiq?

Ans. ____

____

5. Make sentences with:

A. birthday: _____________________________

B. funny : _____________________________

6. What do you want for your birthday and why?

Ans. ____

____

____

____

____

2 The Crows and the Snake

Read the passage and answer the questions that follow:

Long ago, in India, a pair of crows nested in a hollow tree at the bottom of which there lived a snake who used to eat the young birds as soon as they were hatched.

'Oh dear, how can we stop this snake from eating our children?' said the mother crow one day.

'We must get rid of him,' replied the father crow.

'But that is impossible,' said Mrs Crow.

'You know very well that he is much stronger than we are'.

'Don't worry, my dear,' answered her husband. 'Just leave everything to me'.

The following day the king's son came down to a nearby river to swim. When he entered the river to swim, the crow took his gold anklet and dropped it inside the hollow tree in which the crows had their nest.

When he was dressing, the prince noticed his precious anklet was missing. He ordered his servants to search every where. The servants found the anklet in the hollow tree. The servants also found the snake and killed it. The crows were happy and were able to live peacefully.

Questions

1. Where did the crows live?

Ans. ______________________________

2. Who ate the young birds?

Ans. ______________________________

3. Why was it impossible for the crows to get rid of the snake?

Ans. ______________________________

4. Where did the crow drop the anklet?

Ans. ______________________________

5. Who killed the snake?

Ans. ______________________________

6. Find the opposites of the following words from the passage –

i. old ____________ v. weaker ____________

ii. far off ____________ vi. possible ____________

iii. sad ____________ vii. top ____________

iv. lost ____________ viii. night ____________

7. Who was more clever, the father crow or the mother crow?

Ans. ______________________________

8. Write the words used in the passage to describe the nouns –

a. ____________ tree

c. ____________ birds

b. ____________ anklet

d. ____________ river

3 Riddhima and her Doll

Read the passage and answer the questions that follow:

Riddhima was a sweet little five year old girl. One day she did not go to school as it was a holiday. She wore her best dress, took her Barbie doll and went to play in the park nearby. There was a small pond in the park. Ducks and ducklings were swimming in it. Flowers were swaying happily in the cool breeze.

It was a beautiful sight. While she was playing, her doll fell into the water. She started crying because the doll was her favourite toy and was given by her grandmother on her fifth birthday. Vedant who was ten years old waded into the pond and got back the doll for her. Riddhima thanked him and ran back home happily.

Questions

1. Why did Riddhima not go to school?

Ans. ____________________

2. Who had given the doll to Riddhima and when?

Ans. ____

____

3. Why did Riddhima cry?

Ans. ____

____

4. Who got the doll back for Riddhima?

Ans. ____

5. Where were the ducks and ducklings swimming?

Ans. ____

6. Find the opposites of the following words from the passage-

a. Big - ________________ c. Ugly - ________________

b. Warm - ________________ d. Laughing - ________________

7. Make sentences using the following words –

a. favourite - ________________________

b. crying - ________________________

c. happily - ________________________

d. beautiful - ________________________

8. Fill describing words for the following Nouns :

a. ______________, ______________ girl

b. ______________ dress

c. ______________pond

d. ______________breeze

9. Tick (✓) the right answer :

a. Riddhima did not go to school because –

i. it was her birthday ☐

ii. it was a holiday ☐

b. Riddhima went to play –

i. in the park ☐

ii. in the forest ☐

4 The Frogs and the Boys

Read the story and answer the questions that follow:

Some boys were playing near a pond. They picked up some stones and began to throw them into the pond. Stone after stone hit the water.

A family of frogs lived in the pond. They were very frightened. Father Frog said to the family, 'We've got to do something to save ourselves. Let me talk to the boys.'

Father Frog swam to the edge of the pond and said, 'Please stop throwing stones into the pond. You might hurt us.' The boys just laughed and continued to throw stones into the pond.

A farmer was watching all this. He picked up a few small stones. He began to throw them, one at a time, in the direction of the boys.

'Stop! Stop!' cried the boys. 'Can't you see you may hurt us?'

'Why should I stop?' said the farmer. 'Did you stop when you knew that you might hurt the frogs?'

The boys felt ashamed and walked away.

Questions

1. What was the group of boys doing?

Ans. ______________________________

2. Why was the family of frogs frightened?

Ans. ______________________________

____

3. What did the farmer do?

Ans. ______________________________

____

4. What lesson did the boys learn?

Ans. ______________________________

____

5. Write true [T] or false [F] –

   a. The frogs were afraid that the stones would hurt them. [ ]

   b. The farmer threw stones at the frogs. [ ]

   c. The farmer was able to stop the boys from throwing stones into the pond. [ ]

   d. The boys were not ashamed of what they did. [ ]

6. Tick [✓] the right answer –

   a. Father Frog decided to –

      i. fight with the boys. [ ]

      ii. speak to the boys. [ ]

   b. After Father Frog spoke to the boys, they –

      i. stopped throwing stones into the pond. [ ]

      ii. continued to throw stones into the pond. [ ]

   c. The farmer threw stones at the boys –

      i. because he wanted to hurt them. [ ]

      ii. because he wanted to teach them a lesson. [ ]

7. Encircle all the prepositions in the story.

5 The Tenth Boy

Read the passage and answer the questions that follow:

There were ten friends in a village. It was a hot summer morning. So they decided to go for a swim in the river.

The water was nice and cool. Bharat, the leader of the group, said, 'We should be careful. Let's hold hands when we get into the water and stay close to the bank.'

The ten boys got into the river holding hands. But soon they let go of their hands. They splashed around and played happily in the water for a while. When they climbed onto the bank, Bharat said, 'We did not hold hands all the time. We were not careful. Let's find out if all ten of us are safe.'

Bharat made his friends stand in a line. He then began to count, 'One, two, three, four, five, six, seven, eight, nine… Where is the tenth boy?'

A farmer was watching them. He asked Bharat to join the line, and he counted, 'One, two, three, four, five, six, seven, eight, nine, ten! There you are – all of you are safe.'

Bharat said to the farmer, 'Thank you, sir. You helped us find our missing friend.'

Questions

1. Why did the boys decide to go for a swim in the river?

Ans. ____

____

2. Which line in the passage tells you that they enjoyed themselves in the water?

Ans. ____

____

3. Write true [T] or false [F] –

   A. The farmer was a clever person. [ ]

   B. Bharat was not the leader of the group. [ ]

4. Complete the paragraph:

Ans. It was a ______ ________ morning and ______ friends decided to go for a ______ in the river. The water was ______ and ______. Their leader was ______, who asked them to hold their ______ and stay close to the ______.

5. Match the opposites:

a.	friends	careless
b.	hot	unsafe
c.	careful	cold
d.	safe	enemies

6. Make sentences with:

   A. careful : ____________________

   B. happily : ____________________

   C. friends : ____________________

   D. decided : ____________________

7. Tick [✓] the right answer:

   A. The ten friends went for

      a. a swim in the river [ ] b. to play in the park [ ]

   B. The friends

      a. enjoyed their swim [ ] b. did not enjoy their swim [ ]

   C. Bharat counted only nine boys because

      a. one boy was missing [ ] b. he did not count himself [ ]

   D. The tenth boy was

      a. the farmer [ ] b. Bharat [ ]

6 The Emperor's New Clothes

Read the passage and answer the questions that follow:

Once there was an emperor. He ruled over a large kingdom. But he was not a kind king. His people were afraid of him.

He lived in a large palace, and had many horses and carriages. In his palace there were many beautiful things.

One day he heard of a new tailor. People told him that the tailor stitched beautiful clothes.

The tailor told him, 'I'll make a robe for you, Your Highness. It will be a beautiful robe. It will be made of a special kind of cloth. This cloth is very costly. To see the cloth, you have to be a very good person.'

The tailor and his helpers stitched the robe for many days. The emperor gave the tailor lots and lots of money. Nobody could see the cloth. Everyone thought, 'Only good people can see the cloth. I can't see it, but I will say that I can see it.' So they told the emperor, 'The cloth is very fine!'

One day the tailor told the emperor that the robe was ready. He said to the emperor, 'Look at it, Sir. Isn't it beautiful?'

The emperor could see nothing. But he said, 'Yes, it's very beautiful.'

His courtiers too could see nothing. But as they were afraid of him they said, 'Indeed, it's very, very beautiful!'

The tailor helped the emperor to put it on. The emperor went out to show his people his beautiful new clothes. All the people said, 'The emperor's new robe is very beautiful! Long live the emperor!'

Then one little boy from the crowd cried out, 'The emperor isn't wearing any clothes at all! How funny he looks!'

And all the people started laughing. The emperor learnt a lesson and promised to be good to his people.

Questions

1. Why were the people afraid of their emperor?

Ans. ______________________________

2. What did the people tell the emperor about the tailor?

Ans. ______________________________

3. Write three things the tailor told the emperor about the robe.

Ans. ______________________________

____

4. Find the opposites of the words from the passage –

a. ugly - ____________

b. small - ____________

c. cruel - ____________

d. cheap - ____________

e. bad - ____________

5. Write the words used to describe the nouns in the passage –

a. ____________ palace b. ____________ boy

c. ____________ king d. ____________ clothes

6. Complete the sentences –

a. The emperor lived in a large ____________ which had many ____________.

b. The tailor said that the robe would be made of ____________.

c. The tailor said that only good people would be able to ____________.

d. Everybody said that the robe was ____________.

e. Only the little boy said that the emperor wasn't ____________.

7 My Dog, Spot

Read the poem and answer the questions that follow:

I have a white dog
Whose name is Spot
And he's sometimes white
And he's sometimes not.
But whether he's white
Or whether he's not,
There's a patch on his ear
That makes him Spot...

He likes a bone
And he likes a ball
But he doesn't care
For a cat at all.
He waggles his tail.
And he knows what's what,
So I'm glad that he's my dog,
My dog, Spot.

– Rodney Bennett

Questions

1. What colour is Spot?

Ans. ____________________

2. Why is the dog in the poem called Spot?

Ans. ____________________

3. Write two things Spot likes.

Ans. ____________________

4. Does Spot like cats?

Ans. ____________________

5. Find a word in the poem that rhymes with –

Ans. **a.** Spot ____________

b. ball ____________

6. Would you like Spot if he was your dog? Why?

Ans. ____________________

____

____

____

7. Raghav has written a paragraph on 'My Pet' but he has forgotten to write a few words. Help him to complete the paragraph with the help of the words given in the box.

a. love	**b.** morning	**c.** walk	**d.** night	**e.** barks	**f.** guards
g. kennel	**h.** bread	**i.** bones	**j.** pat	**k.** legs	

A. I have a pet dog. His name is Tommy.

B. He eats ____________, meat and ____________.

C. When I ____________ him he stands on his ____________.

D. He sleeps in the ____________.

E. He ____________ at strangers.

F. He ____________ our house at ____________.

G. I take him out for a ____________ every ____________.

H. I ____________ Tommy very much.

8 The Kitten

Read the poem and answer the questions that follow:

I love my little kitten
She has such pretty ways,
She looks so very funny,
When with my ball she plays.

I like to watch my kitten,
She has such funny tricks,
She looks so very pretty,
When paw and fur she licks.

I laugh to see the kitten,
When round and round she runs,
To catch her tail she turns and twists
And yet no near her comes.

Questions

1. Why does the girl love her kitten?

Ans. ______________________________

2. Why does the girl like to watch her kitten ?

Ans. ______________________________

3. Why does the kitten turn and twist?

Ans. ______________________________

4. Find rhyming words from the poem :

a. ways ____________ b. runs ____________ c. licks ____________

5. What are the young ones of the following? You may take help from the box given:

a. Cat ____________ b. Hen ____________

c. Frog ____________ d. Dog ____________

e. Cow ____________ f. Goat ____________

g. Sheep ____________ h. Lion ____________

i. Duck ____________ j. Pig ____________

k. Horse ____________ l. Deer ____________

tadpole	**kid**
kitten	**chicken**
duckling	**fawn**
puppy	**lamb**
piglet	**foal**
cub	**calf**

6. Sounds made by different animals :

A bird - chirps, twitters

A cow - moos

A donkey - brays

A deer - bells

An elephant - trumpets

A crow - caws

A snake - hisses

A sheep - bleats

A wolf - howls

A dog - barks

9 My Computer

Read the poem and answer the questions that follow:

The name of my best friend is Mr Computer.

I have a friend Mr Computer,
He is the best friend I ever had.

He is always ready for work and fun,
And is never cranky or glum.

Always helping me to complete my projects,
With him I play games and do my difficult sums.

I can see cartoons and movies on his screen,
And play games when I come back from school.

My friend makes me learn and play,
As I do with my friends everyday.

Mr Mouse is my friend's pet,
Who helps me to visit the internet.

I scroll the mouse every where,
Then I click left and right,
And it makes things alright.

Mr Computer is my best friend,
He never says no to anything.

Questions

1. Write four things the computer helps the boy to do?

Ans. ____

____

2. Who is his friend's pet? How does the pet help him?

Ans. ____

____

3. Fill the blanks :

1. The computer is your __________ friend.
2. It helps the boy to do his __________ and ________.
3. The boy can watch ________ and play ________ on a computer.
4. Mr ___________ is computer's pet.

4. Write :

1. Any four things you do on your computer at home?

   a. ____

   b. ____

   c. ____

   d. ____

2. Any four places where you see a computer.

   a. ____

   b. ____

   c. ____

   d. ____

5. Match the opposites :

1.	left	-	right
2.	friend	-	never
3.	always	-	easy
4.	difficult	-	enemy

10 The Funny World

Read the poem and answer the questions that follow:

I saw an Elephant
Trying to wipe
The sweat on his trunk
While smoking a pipe!

I saw a Camel
Trying to jump
Right over a hill
That was only his hump!

I saw a Horse
As swift as a gale
Trying to catch up
With its own tail!

I saw a Tiger
Trying to wash
Himself in a tub
Of lemon squash!

Questions

1. Four animals are trying to do funny things. Which animal's action do you find the funniest?

Ans. ____

2. Find words from the poem which rhyme with:

   a. Wash ____________________

   b. Jump ____________________

   c. Wipe ____________________

   d. Gale ____________________

3. In the above poem the poet imagines impossible situations. Do these situations make you laugh?

Ans. ____

____

4. Fill the blanks in Column A with suitable words taken from the pot:

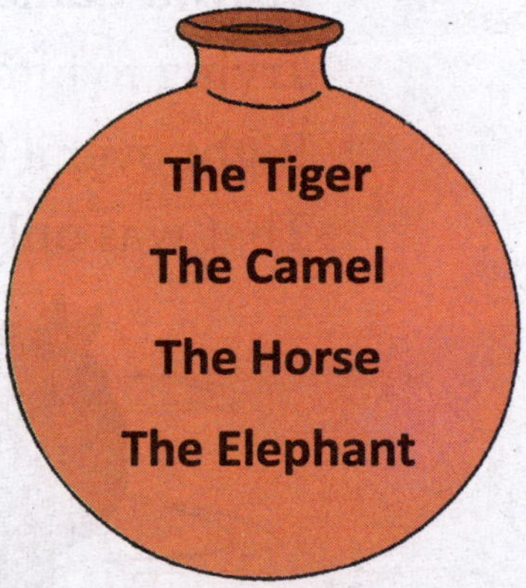

	COLUMN A	COLUMN B
1.	________	wipes the sweat on his trunk
2.	________	was trying to catch its own tail
3.	________	jumps over his hump
4	________	washes himself in a tub of lemon squash

11 The Sentence

Read these words –

wings have birds

Do these words make sense? No, they don't.

Now read the same words in another order –

Birds have wings.

Do these words make sense? Yes, they do.

The words have now been placed in their proper order and they now form a correct sentence. **The sentence makes sense.**

There are two rules to remember when you write a sentence:

1. **A Sentence always begins with a Capital Letter.**
2. **A Sentence always ends with a Full Stop or Question Mark or Exclamation Mark.**

Exercise 1

Radha has not learnt the above rules of a sentence. Help her to write the sentences correctly. The first one has been done for you –

1. raju forgot his lunch box

   Raju forgot his lunch box.

2. apples grow on trees

   ____

3. sunday is a holiday

   ____

4. i live in delhi

   ____

5. the lion slept in the sun

6. it is very cold in winter

Exercise 2

Write the words in the correct order to make sentences. The first one has been done for you –

1. milk, gives, the cow, us

   The cow gives us milk.

2. a, frock, wore, red, the, girl

3. the, sky, shines, in, the, moon

4. months, year, there are, in a, twelve

5. flowers, is, garden, full of, my

6. a bone, was, the dog, chewing

7. a stick, walked, the, with, old man

8. cakes, the little, likes to, girl, eat

9. a walk, took the, Raj, dog, for

10. letters, was, the postman, carrying

12 Naming Words (Nouns)

A policeman

An elephant

A parrot

A park

A pencil box

These are the pictures of a person, an animal, a bird, a place and a thing.

> A Noun is the name of a person, animal, place or thing.
> Nouns are also called **naming** words

Let us play a game. A fairy has lots of naming words in her wings. Write the names under suitable headings:

Write the names here:

Persons	Animals	Birds	Places	Things

Exercise 1

A. Name 5 things in your school bag –

B. Name as many things as you can see in the park –

C. Name the animals you see in the zoo –

D. Name as many things you can see in your class room –

Exercise 2

Fill the blanks with nouns given in the box –

temple, butter, football, carrots, dress, deer, basket, beach, burger, doll

1. Anuj had a ____________ for dinner.
2. Let's play ____________ in the garden.
3. Chavi is going to the __________ for a swim.
4. My grandmother goes to a __________ everyday.
5. The lion killed the __________.
6. The kitten is sleeping in the __________.
7. Divya has a beautiful ____________.
8. The rabbit eats ______________.
9. Raghav puts ____________ on his toast.
10. Mansi wears a blue __________.

Exercise 3

Underline all the nouns in the story and write them in the space given on the next page –

One day a farmer lost his donkey. He went to the king and told him, 'I have lost my donkey.' The king showed him an elephant. He asked, 'Is this your animal?'

The farmer said, 'No, this is an elephant. I have lost a donkey.' The king gave him a donkey. He was very happy.

The next day, a rich farmer went to the king and told him, 'I have lost an animal.'

The king showed him a camel and the farmer said, 'Yes, that is my animal.'

He took the camel and went home. The camel ate all his plants and broke everything in his house. Soon the rich farmer was poor.

____

____

Exercise 4

There are nouns in each sentence given below. Underline them and write them in the space given. One has been done for you –

1. Sheep give us wool. sheep, wool
2. There is a little cat in the garden. ______________
3. The girl has lovely eyes. ______________
4. My father is a doctor. ______________
5. Every child has a book. ______________
6. The monkey loves to eat bananas. ______________
7. The phone is ringing. ______________
8. My school has a big playground. ______________
9. There is a market near my house. ______________
10. My mother took me to the zoo. ______________

Exercise 5

Complete each sentence with a noun –

1. I like to play ______________ with my friends.
2. Rohit has a pet ______________.
3. My mother cooked some tasty ______________ for me.
4. I gave some ______________ to my teacher.
5. Ishita is reading a ______________.
6. The ______________ is dancing.
7. ______________ is sitting in the garden.
8. Rachit loves to drink ______________.
9. My ______________ likes to eat chocolates.
10. Chandan likes to ride his ______________.

13 One and Many (Singular and Plural)

Flower

Flowers

The word 'a flower' means one flower.

When a noun tells us about one person, animal, place or thing, we say it is singular.

The word 'flowers' means more than one flower.

When a noun tells us about two or more people, animals, places or things, we say it is plural.

Exercise 1

Add 's' after each word to make it many. One has been done for you –

1. one bag many **bags**
2. one car many ____________
3. one pin many ____________
4. one net many ____________
5. one pot many ____________

6. one book many ____________

7. one top many ____________

8. one doll many ____________

9. one mat many ____________

10. one cot many ____________

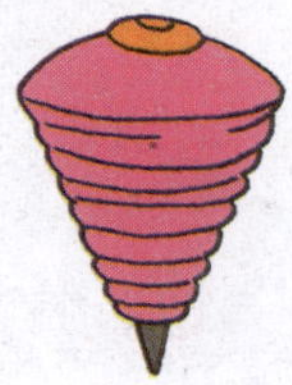

Exercise 2

Add 'es' to the words to make many. One has been done for you –

1. box + es = boxes
2. brush + es = ____________
3. glass + es = ____________
4. watch + es = ____________
5. bus + es = ____________
6. fox + es = ____________
7. dish + es = ____________
8. class + es = ____________
9. match + es = ____________
10. peach + es = ____________

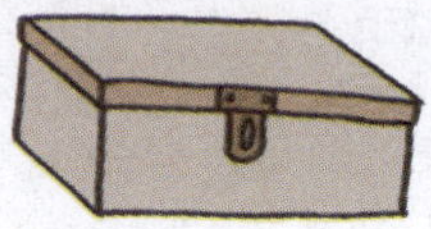

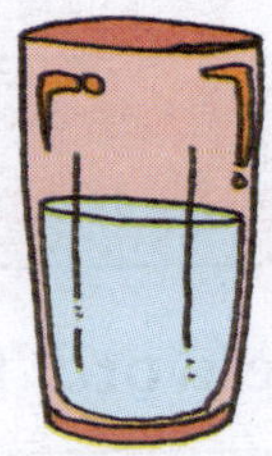

Exercise 3

Fill the blanks with the correct plural of the words given in the brackets –

1. My school has many ____________. (bus)
2. Akshay ate a few ____________. (sweet)
3. Khushi took a basket of ripe ____________ for her aunt. (mango)
4. Neeraj bought some ____________ from the shop. (biscuit)
5. Parul will buy many ____________ from the market. (toy)
6. This shop sells beautiful ____________. (watch)
7. Our holiday ____________ are in this album. (photo)

8. How many ______________ can a rabbit eat? (carrot)

9. The ______________ sat on the tree. (bird)

10. Both ______________ are white. (car)

Exercise 4

Choose the correct word from each pair and underline it –

Megha has invited her friend | friends for her birthday party. Her friends brought many gift | gifts for her. Her mother baked a cake | cakes for the party. Her father put many balloons | balloon and streamers in the room. Her friends played many games | game and ate many tasty snack | snacks.

Exercise 5

Tick the right word from the bracket and rewrite the sentences. The first one has been done for you –

1. I will buy one (dress, dresses) today.

   <u>I will buy one dress today.</u>

2. There are many (cow, cows) in the field.

   ____

3. There is only one (church, churches) in our town.

   ____

4. I have only one (bat, bats).

   ____

5. Several (dish, dishes) were broken.

   ____

6. Many (branch, branches) had no leaves on them.

____

7. There is a (fox, foxes) hiding in the bush.

____

8. We had missed our (train, trains) when we reached the platform.

____

Let us make pairs

For example –

A pair of shoes.

Fill the blanks with the word that fits the best to make a pair. Choose the word from the box –

pail	pair	bar	box	glass	piece	cake	bottle	box	loaf	pile	packet

1. a ________________ of biscuits.
2. a ________________ of chalk.
3. a ________________ of wood.
4. a ________________ of jam.
5. a ________________ of milk.
6. a ________________ of matches.
7. a ________________ of soap.
8. a ________________ of scissors.
9. a ________________ of string.
10. a ________________ of chocolate.
11. a ________________ of water.
12. a ________________ of bread.

14 Animals – Their Homes and Sounds

Animals live in different kinds of homes.

Names of animals are given. Match the animals with their homes. One is done for you:

shed

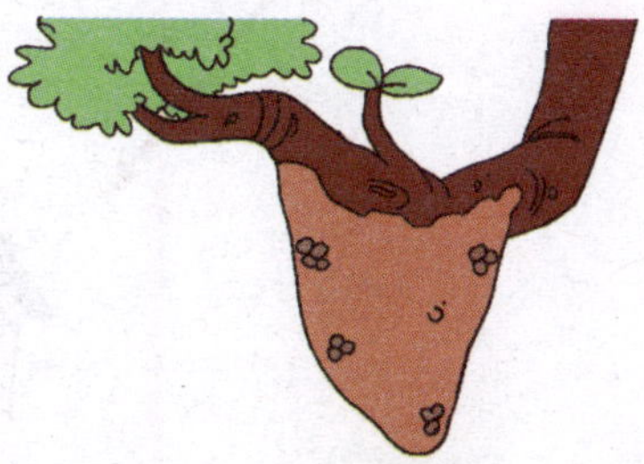

hive

pond

lion

sheep

bird

cow

bees

fish

nest

pen

den

Please find my home :

The following animals have lost their homes. Help them to find their homes. One has been done for you:

Dog			Tree trunk
Owl			Stable
Horse			Kennel
Rabbit		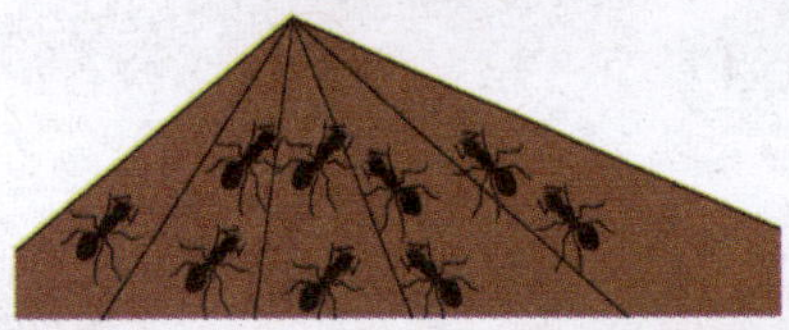	Anthill
Rat			Burrow
Ant			Hole

Learn the sounds that animals make and imitate them:

I Speak, I Say, I Talk

Cats purr.
Lions roar.
Owls hoot.
Bears snore.
Crickets creak.
Mice squeak.
Sheep baa.
But I speak.

Monkeys chatter.
Cows moo.
Ducks quack.
Doves coo.
Pigs squeal.
Horses neigh.
Chickens cluck.
But I say.

Flies hum.
Dogs growl.
Bats screech.
Coyotes howl.
Frogs croak.
Parrots squawk.
Bees buzz.
But I talk.

– Arnold Shapiro

Jack and Jill (Gender)

15

Males (men) are said to be Masculine Gender.
Females (women) are said to be Feminine Gender.

A. Write the Feminine Gender from the box given below :

* princess	* girl
* heroine	* she
* queen	* woman
* wife	* mother
* daughter	* sister
* lady	* grandmother

	Masculine	Feminine
1.	he	________
2.	gentleman	________
3.	boy	________
4.	man	________
5.	brother	________
6.	son	________
7.	father	________
8.	husband	________

9. king __________

10. hero __________

11. prince __________

12. grandfather __________

B. Change the gender of the underlined words and rewrite the sentences :

1. He is a boy.

1. She is a girl.

2. A lady has come.

2. ______________________________

3. The girl is playing.

3. ______________________________

4. The man is working.

4. ______________________________

5. My brother is tall.

5. ______________________________

6. The king wears a crown.

6. ______________________________

7. The hero is dancing.

7. ______________________________

8. My grandfather is old.

8. ______________________________

9. My father has a mobile phone.

9. ______________________________

10. My uncle has two sons.

10. ______________________________

Special Names (Proper Nouns)

16

Every person has a special name. The special name always begins with a capital letter.

For example :

riti verma (wrong) ✗

Riti Verma (right) ✓

Now write :

1. Your name ______________________
2. Your friends' names ______________________

____

____

____

3. Your teacher's name ______________________
4. Your Principal's name ______________________
5. The name of the Prime Minister of India ______________________
6. The name of the President of India ______________________
7. Name of your favourite hero ______________________

8. Your mother's name ______________________

9. Your father's name ______________________

10. Your brother's or sister's name ______________________

All the names you have written above are **special** names.

's (The Apostrophe)

Look at the word – cat's neck

's shows that the neck belongs to the cat.

Complete the following with an apostrophe :

1. A ____________ dress (girl)
2. An ____________ trunk (elephant)
3. The ____________ ball (boy)
4. A ____________ pouch (kangaroo)
5. A ____________ brush (painter)
6. A ____________ nest (bird)
7. A ____________ tail (dog)
8. A ____________ cub (lion)
9. A ____________ sty (pig)
10. The ____________ cradle (baby)

A and An

17

There are 26 letters in the English Alphabet.

There are 5 Vowels. They are:

a e i o u

All the other 21 letters of the alphabet are called Consonants.

We use 'a' before a word beginning with a Consonant.

We use 'an' before a word beginning with a Vowel.

1. an ant
2. a book
3. a car
4. a dog
5. an elephant
6. a frog
7. a girl
8. a hat
9. an ink-pot
10. a jacket
11. a kite
12. a lamp
13. a monkey
14. a net
15. an owl
16. a peacock
17. a queen
18. a rat
19. a star
20. a tub
21. an umbrella
22. a village
23. a watch
24. a xylophone
25. a yo-yo
26. a zebra

We use 'a' and 'an' before nouns which are singular in number.

Look at the pictures below. All these words in the pictures begin with a **vowel.** Use **'an'** before each of these words :-

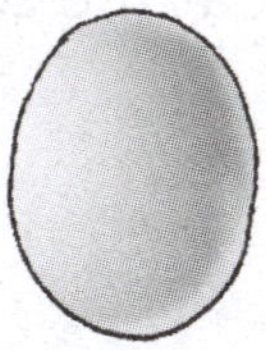

__________ __________ __________ __________ __________

Exercise 1

Put 'a' or 'an' –

1. __________ eye
2. __________ cat
3. __________ ass
4. __________ deer
5. __________ nose
6. __________ inkpot
7. __________ year
8. __________ van
9. __________ owl
10. __________ king
11. __________ insect
12. __________ bin
13. __________ lamp
14. __________ puppy
15. __________ axe
16. __________ elephant
17. __________ ox
18. __________ window
19. __________ hand
20. __________ animal

Exercise 2

Put 'a' or 'an' to complete the sentences –

1. We saw ____ zebra and _____ elephant at the zoo.
2. Rohit ate ____ apple and _____ pear.
3. Mother had _____ cup of tea.
4. Reena put ______egg in the basket.
5. I like to eat ______ ice cream.
6. There is _____ orange and _____ guava on the plate.
7. ______ armchair is ____ piece of furniture.
8. _______ old lady was walking in the park.
9. There is _______empty glass on the table.
10. _______ass and _____ox were in the farm.
11. _____ ugly duckling was in the pond.
12. _____ pilot was flying _____aeroplane.
13. Geeta put ____ letter in ____envelope.
14. _____ elf and ____fairy were seen in fairyland.
15. I saw_____ ostrich in the zoo.

Exercise 3

Put 'a' or 'an' to complete the paragraph –

Ramu is _____ ice-cream seller. One day, he was selling ice-cream when ____ little girl came with ______ elephant. The girl wore _____ blue dress and had _____ orange flower in her hand. She bought _____ ice-cream for herself and _____ bunch of bananas from _____ fruit seller for her elephant.

18 This and That, These and Those

'This' refers to a person or thing near you.

'That' refers to a person or thing far from you.

We use 'this' and 'that' when we speak of one person or thing.

For example –

This is a bat 

That is a cup 

This is a hat 

That is a jug 

A. Put a word for each picture :

1. This is a ________ 
2. This is a ________ 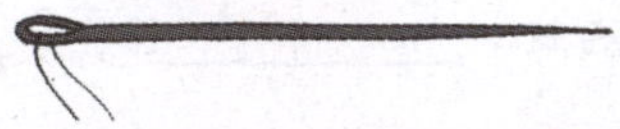
3. That is a ________ 
4. That is a ________ 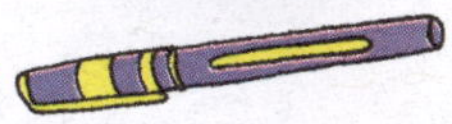
5. This is an ________ 
6. That is an ________ 
7. This is a ________ 
8. That is a ________ 
9. This is a ________ 
10. That is an ________ 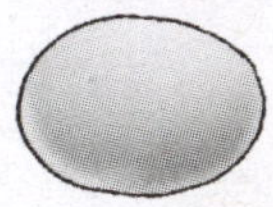

B. Tick (✓) the correct sentence :

1. This is a rat
2. This is a cat
3. This is a mat

1. That is an apple
2. That is an orange
3. That is an egg

1. This is a chair
2. This is a table
3. This is a box

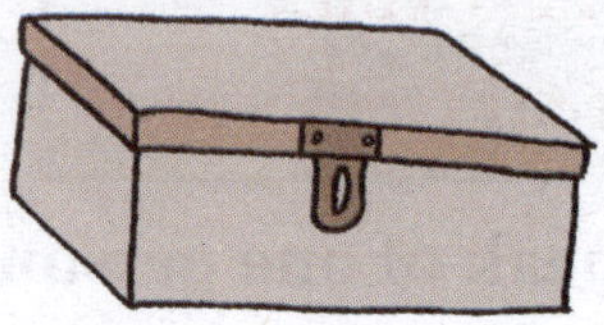

1. That is a hat
2. That is a cap
3. That is a frock

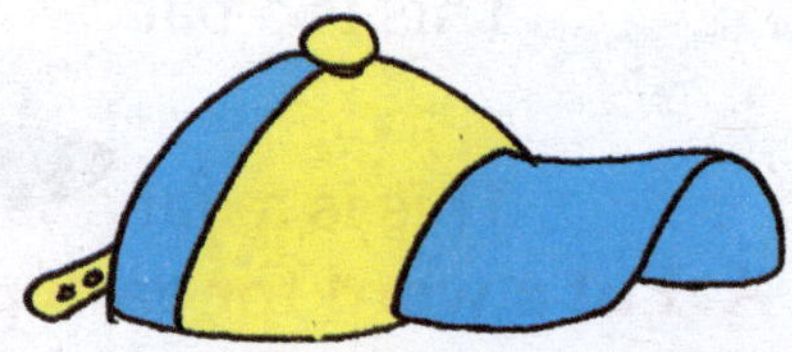

C. Fill the correct words in the blanks :

1. This is a ________ 
2. This is a ________ 
3. This is a ________ 
4. This is a ________ 

1. That is a ________ 
2. That is a ________ 
3. That is a ________ 
4. That is a ________ 

'These' refer to people or things that are near you.
'Those' refer to people or things that are far away from you.

We use 'these' and 'those' when we speak of more than one person or thing.

This (That) is

These (Those) are

This is a tree

These are trees

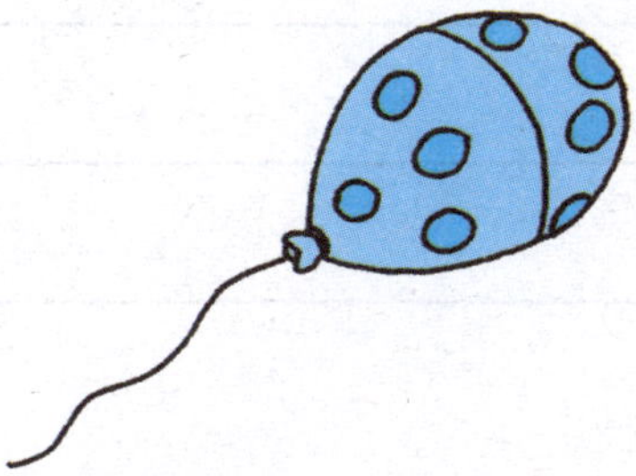

That is a balloon

Those are balloons

This is an ice-cream

These are ice-creams

This is a star

These are stars

A. Now write the following sentences using 'These' and 'Those'. One is done for you :

1.	That is a girl.	1.	Those are girls.
2.	That is an elephant.	2.	________________
3.	That is a cat.	3.	________________
4.	That is a ball.	4.	________________
5.	This is a glass.	5.	________________
6.	This is an egg.	6.	________________
7.	This is an ant.	7.	________________
8.	That is a boy.	8.	________________
9.	This is a puppy.	9.	________________
10.	That is a kite.	10.	________________

B. Picture Reading –

Write the correct words for the pictures :

1. This is a ________ → 

That is a ________ → 

2. This is a ________ → 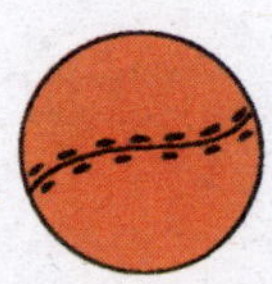

That is a ________ → 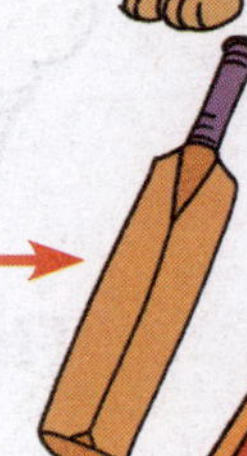

3. This is a ________ → 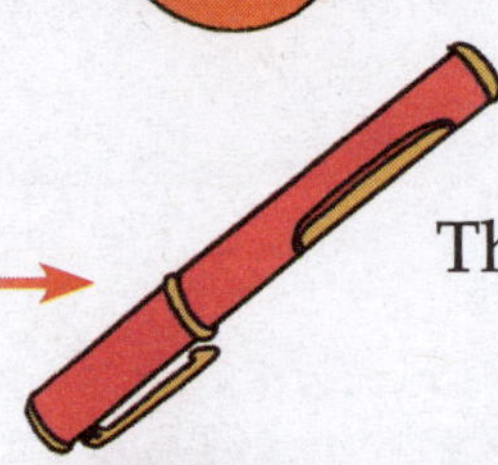

That is a ________ → 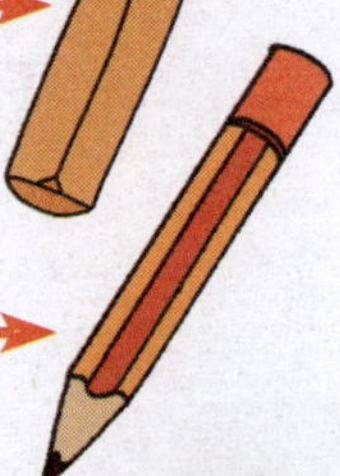

4. This is a ________ → 

That is a ________ → 

19 Opposites

Opposites are Antonyms.

For example – (1) Beautiful – ugly (2) up - down

Exercise 1

Find the opposite words from the box and complete the sentence –

1. Ice is ________ and tea is hot.
2. The ________ cat and the white cat.
3. The ________ boy and the short boy.
4. The ________ shoes and the clean shoes.
5. A ________ day and a dull day.
6. A ________ child and a sad child.
7. A ________ car and a small car.
8. An ________ man and a young boy.
9. Raj is a ________ boy and Rahul is a thin boy.
10. My ________ bag and my new bag.

happy, tall, old, cold, black, big, bright, fat, dirty, big

Exercise 2

Match the opposites and then write them –

right man
son uncle
day first

daughter last
wrong aunt
woman night

1. ____________ ◆ ____________
2. ____________ ◆ ____________

3. ________ ◆ ________

4. ________ ◆ ________

5. ________ ◆ ________

6. ________ ◆ ________

Picture Reading

Look at the pictures and match the sentences:

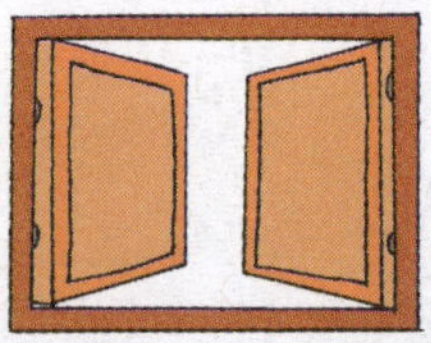

1. The boy is strong	* but the window is open
2. The door is shut	* but the night is cold
3. Rahul is standing	* but the mouse is small
4. The elephant is big	* but the girl is weak
5. The day is hot	* but Radha is sitting

Exercise 3

Write the complete sentences in the space given below.

For example –

1. The boy is strong but the girl is weak.
2. ____________________
3. ____________________
4. ____________________
5. ____________________

Exercise 4

Find opposites of the underlined words and write the sentences again. Choose the words from the box. One has been done for you –

heavy	more	sad	ugly	last	foolish	found	dull	full	sell

1. The princess was <u>beautiful.</u>

   <u>The princess was ugly.</u>

2. Soha carried a <u>light</u> bag.

   ____

3. It is a <u>bright</u> day.

   ____

4. The man was <u>wise</u>.

   ____

5. The box of sweets is <u>empty.</u>

   ____

6. Raj was <u>happy</u> in his new school.

   ____

7. I have <u>lost</u> my book.

   ____

8. Vedant will <u>buy</u> a car.

   ____

9. Kavya came <u>first</u> in the race.

   ____

10. Saumya wants <u>less</u> milk.

   ____

Exercise 5

Look for opposites in the crossword given below. The first one has been done for you –

1.	Tall	-	________	**6.**	Wild	-	________
2.	Large	-	________	**7.**	Top	-	________
3.	Wrong	-	________	**8.**	Hot	-	________
4.	New	-	________	**9.**	Clean	-	________
5.	Heavy	-	________	**10.**	Fat	-	________

20

Action Words (Verb)

A word that shows an action is called an action word or a VERB.

For example –

eat, sleep, sing, play, run, dance, carry, bend, swim, are all action words.

Put the right action word or doing word under each picture.

You may take help from the action words given in the box :

____

____

____

____

____

____

____

____

____

____

____

____

write	sing	read	sleep	drink	swim
cut	eat	kick	play	run	draw

What is Tanvi doing?

Tanvi is a very active girl. She does a number of activities.

Complete each sentence with the right doing word (verb) from the box. All the doing words end in **'ing'** :

standing	sleeping	reading	skipping	writing	sitting
eating	playing	walking	going	drinking	painting

Tanvi is ______________ a letter.

Tanvi is ______________ in her bed.

Tanvi is ______________ a book.

Tanvi is ______________ bread.

Tanvi is______________ a rope.

Tanvi is ______________ near the tree.

Tanvi is ______________ to school.

Tanvi is ______________________ .

Tanvi is ___________ .

Tanvi is ____________ .

Tanvi is _________ on a chair.

Tanvi is ___________ milk.

Is, Am, Are –

Is is used for singular number (one)

For example : She **is** a girl.

Are is used for plural number (many)

For example : They **are** children.

With **'I'** we use **'am'**

For example – __I am__ a boy.

Exercise 1

Fill the blanks with is, am or are –

1. I ______ a good girl.
2. These ______ frogs.
3. Rakhi ______ dancing.
4. We ______ playing.
5. Grass ______ green.
6. Neha ______ climbing the tree.
7. They ______ my friends.
8. Those roses ______ beautiful.
9. My name ______ Jhanvi.
10. I ______ five years old.
11. It ______ a bright day today.
12. He ______ an old man.
13. She ______ my best friend.
14. I ______ reading a book.
15. They ______ going to school.

Exercise 2

Fill the blanks with verbs given in the box –

making	writing	drinking	singing	eating
sleeping	reading	playing	running	swimming

1. I like ____________ sand castles on the beach.
2. The baby is ________________.
3. Tanya likes ______________ her story book.
4. Shashank is ______________ a letter.
5. The children are ______________ in the park.

6. Manan is ________________ orange juice.
7. Charu is ______________ on stage.
8. Madhur is ______________ an apple.
9. Sandy is _____________ in the playground.
10. The duck is ______________ in the pond.

Exercise 3

Circle the verbs in the following sentences –

1. The man climbs the mountains.
2. The lion sleeps in the bushes.
3. Arpita plays the guitar.
4. The farmer plants the seeds.
5. Jack and Jill went up the hill.
6. Mother cooks dinner for us.
7. The boy kicks the ball.
8. The maid washes the clothes.
9. The stars shine at night.
10. The fish swim in the pond.

Exercise 4

Can you say what the following do? Choose the correct answer –

1. Dogs ___________ their tails. (wag, shake)
2. Hens ___________ eggs. (lay, give)
3. Artists __________ pictures. (paint, cook)
4. Children ____________ kites. (make, fly)
5. Bells _______________ loudly. (blow, ring)
6. Aeroplane __________ in the sky. (sails, flies)

Exercise 5

The Elephant and the Tailor

Complete the story with the help of verbs given in the box –

lifts	give	sees	eats	gives	get	throws	passes	waves	goes

Jumbo the elephant ________ for a bath in the river. He ________ a tailor's shop. Ali the tailor ________ him a banana. Jumbo _______ the banana. He is happy. He __________ his trunk.

The next day Jumbo ________ Ali's shop. Ali gives him a stone. Jumbo _________ it away. Jumbo comes back from the river and _______ his trunk. He throws water on Ali. Ali's clothes _________ wet. Ali says, 'Sorry, Jumbo! I'll _________ you a banana tomorrow'.

21 'Was' and 'Were'

Look at the picture, and then read the sentences:

1. There was a girl.
2. The girl was tall.
3. There were two boys.
4. The boys were short.

We use 'was' when we speak about one person or thing.
We use 'were' when we speak about more than one person or thing.

Exercise 1

Fill the blanks with 'was' or 'were' –

1. The flight __________ late.
2. Her clothes __________ dirty.
3. Advitya __________ present in school today.
4. Those girls __________ making a noise.
5. The baby __________ sleeping in the cot.
6. Saturday __________ a holiday.
7. The children __________ playing games on the computer.
8. Chandan and his friends __________ waiting for a bus.

Exercise 2

Fill the blanks with 'There was' or 'There were' –

1. __________________ many cows in the fields.
2. __________________ a picture on the wall.
3. __________________ eleven players in the team.
4. __________________ clouds in the sky.
5. __________________ three kittens in the farm.
6. __________________ a bike in the street.
7. __________________ no chairs in the room.
8. __________________ many flowers in the garden.

'Has' and 'Have'

22

Look at the picture, and then read the sentences:

1. The boy has a bat in his hand.
2. The boys have bats in their hands.
3. The boy has new shoes.
4. The boys have new shoes.

We use 'has' when we speak about one person or thing.

We use 'have' when we speak about more than one person or thing.

Exercise 1

Fill the blanks with 'has' or 'have' –

1. Ananya __________ a new pair of socks.
2. An ant __________ six legs.
3. __________ you been here before?
4. The room __________ two doors and four windows.
5. How many days __________ February?
6. A butterfly __________ wings.
7. Tom and Lily __________ a pony.
8. The tree __________ red flowers.
9. I __________ a rupee in my pocket.
10. We __________ a baby lamb in our garden.
11. Did you __________ milk and toast for breakfast.
12. __________ you a clock at home?
13. The boy __________ a bat and a ball.
14. Surbhi __________ blue eyes.
15. My uncle __________ two daughters.

23

The Right Word

Given below are eight naming words (nouns):

knife chalk brush key broom scales spade needle

And there are eight action words (verbs):

cuts paints opens sews sweeps digs weighs writes

Each of these sentences has one noun and one verb. Write the correct words in the sentences. The first one has been done for you –

1. Madhur ___cuts___ the mango with a ___knife___ knife .
2. The teacher __________ on the board with __________.

3. The tailor __________ the frock with a __________.
4. The maid __________ the floor with a __________.
5. Father __________ the front door with a __________.

6. The gardener __________ his garden with a __________.
7. The grocer __________ the sugar on his __________.
8. The painter __________ the wall with a __________.

Words used in place of Nouns (Pronouns)

24

Words which are used instead of Nouns are called Pronouns.

We use Pronouns:

'He', 'Him', 'His' for a boy or a man.

'She', 'Her' for a girl or a woman.

'It' for a place, animal or thing.

'I', "We', 'Me', 'Us', 'You', 'Your', 'They',

'Them', 'Their' for boys, girls, men or women.

'They', 'Them', 'Their' for persons, places or animals.

Exercise 1

Underline the pronouns in the following sentences –

1. You are a good boy, Raj. I like you. Let us play in the park.
2. I am Rahul. I am playing with my friends.
3. I am a girl. Look at me and my friend, Radha.
4. He is our teacher. Let us meet him.
5. This is a flower. Smell it.
6. My uncle bought chocolates for us.
7. I met a man. He was riding a horse.
8. Arif said to me, 'I want to talk to you.'
9. The children are playing with their friends.
10. Akshay, you are a lazy boy. You never complete your work.

Exercise 2

Circle the pronouns in the story –

A cat and a dog were good friends. They played together everyday.

'I am so happy you are my friend', the cat and the dog said to each other.

One day the cat said, 'It is hot.' 'No! It is cold,' said the dog.

Soon they started fighting and stopped being friends. They did not play together anymore. This made them sad.

An owl saw them and asked, 'Why are you not playing together?

Don't you know that is it hot in the sun and cold in the shade?'

They looked at each other. They realized they should not fight.

'Let us be friends again,' they both said together.

Exercise 3

Fill the blanks with pronouns –

1. _____ am a boy.
2. Put away the toys or ______will get lost.
3. I call my dog Jojo. _____ loves _____.
4. We went for a picnic with my cousins. ____ had brought a lot of food.
5. The children are playing in the park. _____ are making a lot of noise.
6. Neeta has a farm.____ is very big.
7. Reena's mother gave ______ a blue cap.
8. Kush and Parth like swimming. ______ go to the pool everyday.
9. Rohan has a pet parrot.____ gives ____ seeds.
10. Nitin bought a new bat. ____ likes playing with ____.

Exercise 4

Rewrite the following sentences using pronouns instead of the words in blue –

1. Raj met Ali. Raj spoke to Ali.
1. Raj met Ali. He spoke to him.
2. Mehak met Varis. Mehak gave Varis a toy.
2. ____

3. Tanvi is a good girl. Tanvi does all her work. All the teachers like Tanvi.
3. ____
4. Where are the books? The books are on the table.
4. ____

5. See these trees. The trees have many apples on the trees.
5. ____
6. I like grapes. Grapes are sweet.
6. ____

25 Word Puzzle

A. Fill the word puzzle. For each clue, think of a word containing the letters 'oa' –

1. Sound of lion.  1

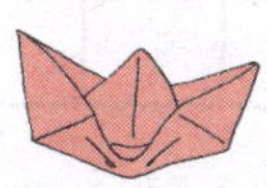

2. In rainy season, children make paper. 2

3. We wear it in winters. 3

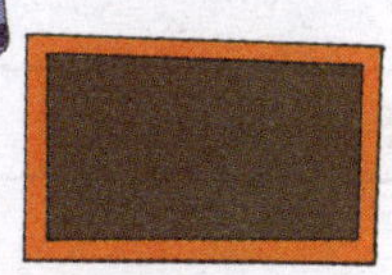

4. My teacher writes on it. 4

5. I spread butter or jam on it. 5

6. Traffic moves on it. 6

7. We use it for a bath. 7

8. A frog like animal. 8

9. Its baby is called a kid. 9

B. These are clues of the people who help us. Can you find their names? One has been done for you –

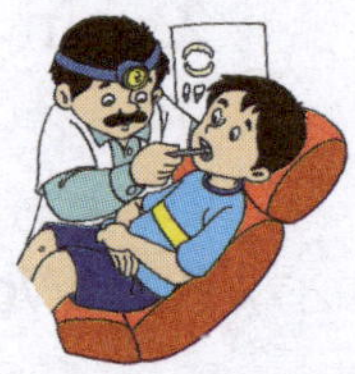

No.	Clue							
1.	I bake bread.	B	A	K	E	R		
2.	I plough the land.	F			M		R	
3.	I cut your hair.	B		R			R	
4.	I sell tea and sugar.	G			C		R	
5.	I look after your teeth.	D			T			T
6.	I put out fires.	F		R				N
7.	I treat sick people.	D			T		R	
8.	I mend your shoes.	C			B			R
9.	I bring your letters.	P			T			N
10.	I sweep the streets.	S		E				R

26 Describing Words (Adjectives)

Words which describe persons, places, things or animals are called describing words.

Complete the following with the help of the words given in the box :

a ________ girl a ________ girl a________ boy a ________ boy

_______ coffee _________ coffee a ______ animal a ______ animal

  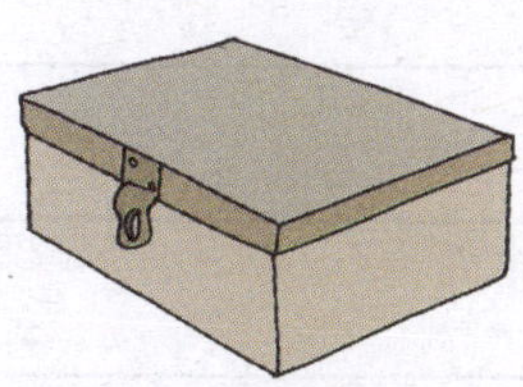 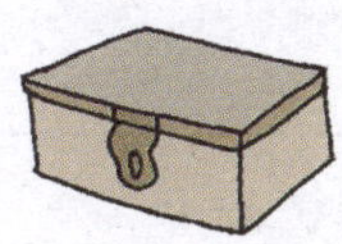

a _______ lake a ________ lake a ________ box a ________ box

short thin large big heavy tall fat hot small tiny light cold

Describing words come before a naming word or a noun.

For example –

1. a red rose
2. a long stick
3. an old man
4. a big garden

Activity 1

Children are asked to describe their mother.

Write 5 sentences about your mother :

____

____

____

____

____

Activity 2

Children are asked to describe the cartoon character Noddy.

Write 5 sentences about Noddy :

____

____

____

____

____

Activity 3

Children are asked to describe a doll.

Write 5 sentences about a doll :

____

____

____

____

____

____

Exercise 1

Match the describing words :

1. bright	dirty
2. hard	soft
3. fat	empty
4. clean	sad
5. fast	bitter
6. full	tame
7. wild	kind
8. cruel	dull
9. happy	thin
10. sweet	slow

Exercise 2

Complete the sentences with the help of words given in the box :

1. an old woman and a ______________ woman
2. a big plant and a ________________ plant
3. a heavy box and a ________________ box
4. a rich man and a ________________ man
5. a strong man and a ______________ child

weak	poor	light	small	young

Exercise 3

Underline the adjectives in the sentences –

1. Vedant likes to eat creamy, chocolate biscuits.
2. I picked some lovely, colourful flowers for my mother.
3. Soni likes to eat fresh, cheese sandwiches.

4. The puppy is playful and naughty.
5. The man wore a blue shirt and a black coat.
6. Ratik wore a red and white dress.
7. There is a tall, green, shady tree in the park.
8. Rabbits like to eat juicy, red carrots.
9. We went on a picnic on a bright and sunny day.
10. I tried to open the heavy, wooden door.

Exercise 4

Fill the blanks with adjectives and write the words in the puzzle given below–

1. a r______ rose.
2. a b_______ bee.
3. a pr_______ girl.
4. a t________ boy.
5. a s_______ pillow.
6. a f______ man.

Exercise 5

Circle the words on each line that could describe the noun –

1. apple	round	juicy	red	sweet
2. puppy	soft	playful	hungry	fresh
3. cake	tasty	fresh	plastic	sweet
4. mouse	tiny	soft	brown	tall
5. flower	tasty	lovely	pretty	beautiful

In What Position? (Preposition)

27

A Preposition shows relationship between words in a sentence.

Riddhima's puppy Poopsie is very naughty. It loves to go here and there.

in the box

on the table

behind the tree

under the table

near the bed

between the trees

in front of the car

jumping over the hedge

running across the road

below his picture

playing with the ball

Exercise 1

Put the missing words –

1. The cat is __________ the box.
2. The clock is __________ the door.
3. The dog is __________ the kennel.
4. The mouse is ___________ the table.
5. The boy is ______________ the tree.
6. Ritu is sitting ___________ the chair.
7. The children are playing _____________ a ball.
8. Rohan is standing __________ his sisters.
9. The birds are flying ___________ the tree.
10. The doll is ____________ the bed.

Exercise 2

Tick the right (✓) answer –

1. The cat is
   a. between the girls
   b. in front of the girls
   c. behind the girls

2. Reena is walking
   a. before her mother
   b. between her mother
   c. behind her mother

3. The bird is flying
   a. under the tree
   b. over the tree
   c. on the tree

4. The doll is
   a. near the table
   b. under the table
   c. behind the table

5. The picture is
   a. on the wall
   b. above the wall
   c. below the wall

Exercise 3

Fill the blanks with the correct prepositions from the brackets –

1. Open your book_____ page 10. (on, to)
2. The policeman is __________ duty. (on, at)
3. Rama spoke ___________ Anuradha. (with, to)
4. Praveen sang _________ the concert. (in, at)
5. Sunita was walking __________ a friend. (to, with)
6. The cat jumped ____________ the well. (in, into)
7. The lion ran __________ the deer. (before, after)
8. The stadium was full __________ people. (with, of)
9. Sangeeta went to the cinema _________ Suman. (by, with)
10. Meenu cuts the cake _____________ a knife. (with, from)

Exercise 4

Fill the blanks with the correct prepositions from the box to complete the paragraph –

Devika and Sanya were going _____ their grandparents house ______ the holidays. They were going ________ their Mummy and Papa. They were going _____ train. When they reached the railway station, they got ________ the train. Devika sat next to the window. The train started moving. Sanya played ________ her doll. The train went __________ a bridge. It made a lot _____ noise. Devika looked out _____ the window. She saw cows, trees and fields. The train went _________ a tunnel. It became dark. Devika and Sanya screamed loudly!

over	into	of	with	to	into	by	with	for	of

28 Riddles

Solve the riddles with the help of answers given in the box. The first one has been done for you –

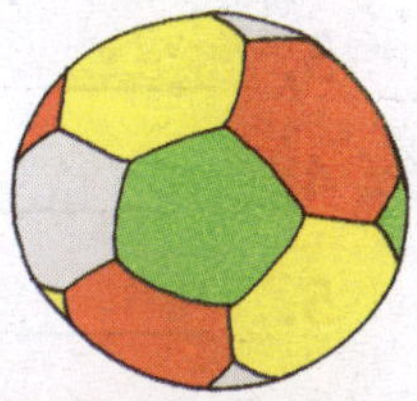
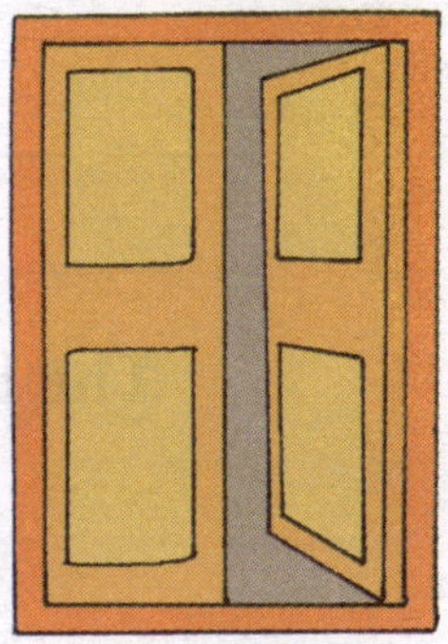
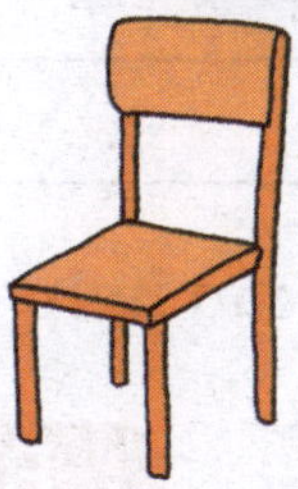
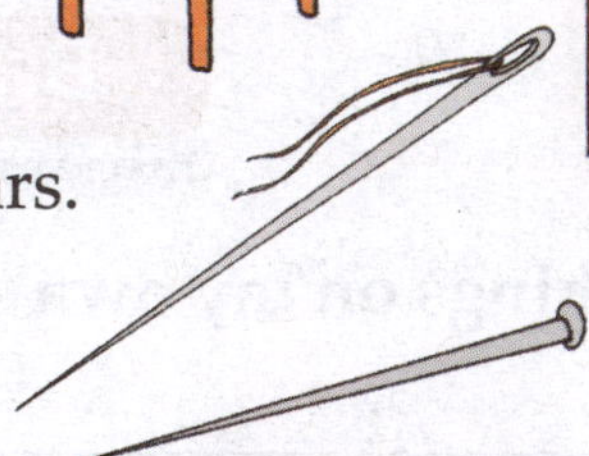

1. It can swim, but cannot walk.
   What is it? ______It is a fish.______
2. It has two hands, but cannot hold anything.
   What is it? ____________________
3. It is kicked many times, but never cries.
   What is it? ____________________
4. It has a tongue, but cannot talk.
   What is it? ____________________
5. It takes many a knock, but never cries.
   What is it? ____________________
6. It has four legs, but cannot walk.
   What is it? ____________________
7. It has an eye, but cannot see.
   What is it? ____________________
8. It has a head, but it has no eyes and no ears.
   What is it? ____________________
9. It is not a bird, but it can fly in the sky.
   What is it? ____________________
10. It has a trunk, but it never packs it.
    What is it? ____________________

door, pin, fish, shoe, football, elephant, clock, chair, needle, aeroplane

Creative Writing

29

A. My Best Friend

With the help of the words given in the box, frame sentences about your best friend:

plays, helps me, share, tiffin, study, games, helpful, toffees, birthday

I love my friend because

1. ____________________

2. ____________________

3. ____________________

4. ____________________

5. ____________________

6. ____________________

7. ____________________

8. ____________________

The teacher can help children to frame the above sentences.

B. What can I do

I can do many things on my own

1. I can ____________________

2. I can ____________________

3. I can ____________________

4. I can also do ____________________

5. I sometimes do ____________________

With things I need help ____________________

1. I need help to ____________________
2. I also need help to ____________________

Things I cannot do ____________________

1. I cannot ____________________
2. I cannot ____________________

C. What I would like to be?

A Computer Engineer

A doctor

A Pilot

A Film Star

A Teacher

A Police Officer

D. Write about Yourself?

Do you want to be something else? Write what you would like to be and why?.

____

____

____

____

E. Let us Play a Game

Write the names of five friends and ask them what they would like to be:

	Name	What he/she would like to be
1.	______________	________________________
2.	______________	________________________
3.	______________	________________________
4.	______________	________________________
5.	______________	________________________

F. My Pet

You have got a puppy from your father. How will you take care of him? Read the questions and write your answers to form a paragraph.

- What name will you give to your puppy?
- What does it look like?
- What will you give him to eat?
- Where will he sleep?
- How will you keep him clean?
- What games will you play with him?

____

____

____

____

____

____

30 Picture Composition

A. Our Family

- What is Grandmother doing? ______________________
- Who is playing with the wool? ______________________
- What are Neha and Rahul doing? ______________________
- What are father and mother having? ______________________
- What is grandfather doing? ______________________
- What is the colour of the house? ______________________

B. A Picnic

Look at the pictures. Write the words given in the box and complete the story –

sun tree mango snacks garden flowers trees parrot

In the holidays Arya, Bhumi amd Megha went to a _______. The garden was full of lovely _______ and tall ________. The ________ was shining. The girls played many games and enjoyed themselves. Then they were hungry. They sat under a mango ________ to eat their tasty ________. Suddenly a _________ fell on them. As they looked up they saw a ________ sitting on the tree. The girls laughed loudly and ate the mango also.

C. Leena's Tiffin Box

Look at the pictures. Write the words and complete the story –

One morning Leena took her new tiffin box to _________. 

In the playground, the _________ 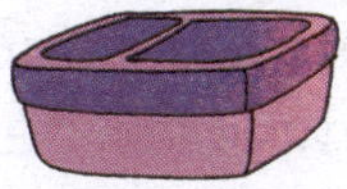 fell out of her _____________.  A ___________  saw the tiffin box, picked it up between its teeth and ran away with it. Leena turned and chased the puppy. The puppy ran across the ___________.  Suddenly the puppy dropped the tiffin box and began eating the tasty _____________  and ____________.  Leena's teacher picked up the tiffin box and said to her, 'It seems the puppy is very hungry and likes the food in your ________________. 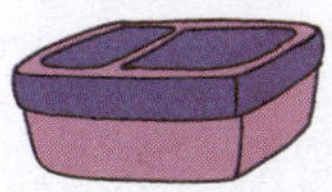 She gave an ______________  and an ______________ 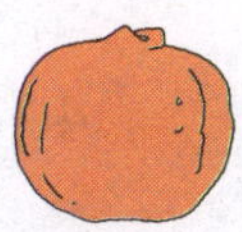 to Leena. Leena thanked her teacher and joined her _________. 

D. Banana Split

Devika was making banana split. She wanted to send the recipe to her cousin Riddhima. She forgot to write a few words. Assist her to complete the recipe with the help of the words given in the box.

You will need:

1 banana
2 scoops of ice-cream
Chocolate sauce
A few strawberries
Some chocolate chips

What to do:

1. Peel the ____________ and cut it down the ____________, from the _______ to the _________.

2. Put the banana on a __________ and put the _____________ on top of it.

3. Pour the ______________ sauce over the banana and ice-cream.

4. Put the __________ and chocolate ______ on the _________.

Your Banana Split is now ready to eat!

chocolate	**plate**	**chips**	**top**	**banana**
strawberries	**ice-cream**	**bottom**	**middle**	**top**

E. Happy Birthday Neha!

- Whose birthday is it? ________________________________

- What is mother doing? ________________________________

- Who is enjoying the party? ________________________________

- Where is the cake? ________________________________

- How many candles are there on the cake? ________________________________

- How old is Neha? ________________________________

F. The Stolen Ring

Look at the pictures. Write the words and complete the story –

A  ________ went to a  ________ and bought a  ________. She paid a lot of  ________ for it. When she went to her  ________ at night, she put it on a  ________ near the  ________. In the  ________ a  ________ hopped into the  ________, saw the ring and flew away with it. When the  ________ woke up, there was no  ________ on the  ________. She at once picked up the  ________ and rang up the  ________. 'A  ________ has stolen my  ________,' she said. 'Please come to my  ________ at 51 Vivek Vihar quickly.'

Soon two  ________ arrived. They looked everywhere in the  ________ but they could not find the  ________. At last one of the  ________ asked the lady, 'Was the  ________ open?' 'Yes, it was,' said the  ________. When the police men looked out of the window, they saw a  ________ lying near it. Then they saw a big, black  ________ flying to a ________  nearby. There was a bird's  ________ on a  ________ of the  ________. One of the  ________ at once climbed up the  ________. He put his  ________ inside the  ________ and pulled out the ring and gave it to the lady. The  ________ thanked the  ________.